MORE THAN ORDINARY
faith:
why does God allow suffering?

KIT AND DREW COONS

More Than Ordinary Faith: Why Does God Allow Suffering?

© 2018 Kit and Drew Coons

ISBN: 978-0-9995689-4-1

All rights reserved. No part of this publication may be reproduced or transmitted in any form or by any means, electronic, mechanical, including photocopy, recording, or any information storage and retrieval system, without permission from the publisher. Requests for permission to make copies of any part of this publication should be sent to: https://morethanordinarylives.com/

Unless otherwise noted, all Scripture quotations are taken from the New American Standard Bible (NASB). Copyright © 1960, 1962, 1963, 1968, 1971, 1972, 1973, 1975, 1977, 1995 by The Lockman Foundation

Edited by Jayna Richardson
Design: Julie Sullivan (MerakiLifeDesigns.com)

First Edition

Printed in the United States

22 21 20 19 18   1 2 3 4 5

contents

The Question We All Ask 1

Suffering is a Part of Life 5
    A Shallow Interpretation

God's Purposes for Suffering 9
    Suffering that God Allows for a Higher Purpose
    Suffering that God Allows People to Bring on Themselves or Others

Biblical Responses to Suffering 33

God is Good................................. 49

THE QUESTION
we all ask

Drew: On Tuesday nights, we did visitation for our church. Because Kit and I had missionary experience, our pastor split us up. Each of us took another man and woman to train them. At one home, tragedy in the form of the unexpected death of a loved one had brought great grief. "Why does God allow suffering?" a tearful lady asked.

I had just finished an in-depth Bible study on God's purposes for suffering. I'm ready for this, I thought and eagerly started explaining the biblical causes of *suffering. I hardly noticed that the lady's expression became glazed, perhaps even stunned. My woman trainee noticed, though. She went to sit by the grieving woman and hugged her. She gave her sympathy and comfort. The lady visibly looked better. That night I was the trainee.*

Why does God allow suffering? This is a universal question in every culture and in every heart. And the question is reasonable and valid. Lack of a meaningful answer is a barrier to the faith of many. Shallow answers can undermine faith. Fortunately, the Bible gives clear reasons that God allows suffering.

But people in intense grief are not looking for theology. They need comfort. However, when we already know the theology behind suffering, God can use it to comfort us when difficulties come. Therefore, the best time to discover God's reasons is *before* a crisis arises and causes faith to waver. This Bible-based mini-book and discussion guide will explore God's purposes for suffering. We can prepare now for the heartaches that are an inevitable part of life.

> The root of all sin is the suspicion that God isn't good. And t's the traumas of life that cause us to question it.[1] (Oswald Chambers)

Suffering can take many different forms. A physical affliction or illness causes suffering. Severe emotional suffering can come after a tragedy. Or suffering can be the trauma of fear and uncertairty in difficult circumstances. One of the most difficult circumstances to bear can be feeling helpless when a loved one suffers. Whatever form suffering takes, trusting God can be a challenge.

> Kit: As we struggled to have children, I could not help noticing our friends getting pregnant. Drew, trying to be an encouragement, said to me, "Anyone can have a baby." He further explained that other aspects of life could be more important. I only heard the "Anyone can have a baby" and thought, "Anyone but ME!" Such feelings may cause us to doubt God. Unwanted pregnancies by married couples, unwed mothers, and the many aborted babies added to my doubt. Being different from everyone around you is frustrating, painful, and just plain not fun. We start asking ourselves, "Why does God allow this?" and "Does God even care?"

Everyone fears suffering and loss for themselves and their loved ones. Even Jesus momentarily knew fear of suffering. On the Mount of Olives he prayed, "Father, if you are willing, remove this cup from me." (Luke 22:42) Verse 44 describes Jesus as "being in agony" before the coming ordeal. Jesus concluded with the prayer, "Yet not my will, but yours be done." He demonstrated great faith by trusting God and His purpose despite fears.

> "When that injury struck you and you thought everything was gone, did you so trust in God that you came out richer than you went in?"[2] (Mrs. Charles E. Cowman)

The purpose of this mini-book is to learn about suffering from a biblical perspective. We believe that knowledge of God's purposes can result in more than ordinary faith. Practical suggestions of steps to take while suffering will also be covered. Since suffering is such a universal question, we have specifically designed this material to be easily adapted to a Bible study using discussion questions. If studying as a couple, individual, or group, please take time to think through your responses to the questions after each section.

Questions for Thought

What types of suffering can cause people to question God?

How can the issue of suffering cause us to doubt God's plan for our lives?

Why is observing the suffering of others sometimes the most severe type of suffering?

SUFFERING IS A *part of life*

Many people's goal is to go through life as pain-free as possible. If that's your attitude, we've got bad news. A pain-free life is not necessarily God's will for us. The disciples of Jesus would be quick to remind us that pain and suffering are part of Christianity. To suffer was a natural part of following Jesus. We tend to like the "power of His resurrection" of Philippians 3:10, but we conveniently forget about sharing the "fellowship of His sufferings." The disciples were surprised not when they *did* experience suffering, but when they *didn't*.

> . . . *that I might know Him, and the power of His resurrection, and the fellowship of His sufferings, being conformed to His death. (Philippians 3:10)*

We 21st-century American Christians have lost our historical perspective. For nearly 2,000 years, those in desperate circumstances, those suffering, have most readily embraced the gospel of Christ. That is still true across most of our world. The downtrodden have always been receptive because Christ offers them a better life to come. But the message of Christ also offers a means in this life to deal with tragic circumstances.

> The person who expects to escape the pangs of suffering and disappointment simply has no knowledge of the Bible, of history, or of life.[3] (Billy Graham)

> *Beloved, do not be surprised at the fiery ordeal among you, which comes upon you for your testing, as though some strange thing were happening to you; but to the degree that you share the sufferings of Christ, keep on rejoicing, so that also at the revelation of His glory you may rejoice with exultation. (1 Peter 4:12-13)*

A Shallow Interpretation

> *And we know that God causes all things to work together for good to those who love God, to those who are called according to His purpose. (Romans 8:28)*

Frequently, you hear Romans 8:28 used as a general explanation for suffering. Usually the verse is followed by an anecdotal story about circumstances having worked out unexpectedly for the best of those involved. We've even heard public readings of this verse in which each person inserted their name: "All things work together for the good of Drew." However, guaranteeing a personal application of this verse in this life can create unbiblical expectations. Sufferers may be disheartened when no apparent benefit appears or doesn't seen adequate to merit the degree of suffering.

God can and frequently does use suffering for the benefit of individuals. Drew shares personal stories in *More Than Ordinary Wisdom* of how God used undesirable situations to teach him important lessons.

But history tells us that many Christians have died miserable deaths from starvation, torture, murder, or plague, or have seen their loved ones experience horrible suffering and death. The circumstances did not work out for the specific good of those individuals *in this life*. We personally believe that those who die thusly will be shown how their suffering benefited those left behind. The good they receive would be the hereafter joy of being part of God's eternal purpose. Yet in many tragic examples of suffering and death, we cannot discern how the victim as an individual could possibly benefit in this life.

Rather, we believe the best interpretation of Romans 8:28 is that God has an ultimate plan for mankind. All of God's creation is working toward the ultimate good of God's children. God knows and experiences our pain. Nevertheless, the Bible describes these troubles as "momentary, light affliction" (2 Corinthians 4:17) in comparison to God's eternal purpose. God takes the eternal view.

Questions for Thought

Have you seen situations when someone used Romans 8:28 in an insensitive manner?

What do you think about the "ultimate plan" interpretation?

How could a shallow answer to the causes of suffering produce more doubt?

How could confidence that the Bible gives meaningful reasons for suffering be an antidote to doubt?

GOD'S PURPOSES *for suffering*

Unbelievers sometimes ask, "How could anyone trust in a God who allows so much suffering?" If you choose not to trust in God, that's a convenient, noble-sounding reason. But "so much suffering" is relative. Living in Africa, we saw many suffering the effects of polio, blindness due to measles, AIDS, and leprosy. To them, the suffering most people experience in America might seem less traumatic.

A more valid question is when Christians ask, as Gideon did in Judges 6:13, "If the Lord is with us, why then has all this happened to us?" They reason, "As a parent, I would never willingly allow my children such heartache. Why does our heavenly Father?" These often-unspoken questions can undermine our faith and render us ineffective for our Lord. God didn't rebuke Gideon for asking, but God had to build Gideon's faith through some remarkable signs. For us, God has given the Scriptures to build our faith.

> *For whatever was written in earlier times was written for our instruction, so that through perseverance and the encouragement of the Scriptures we might have hope. (Romans 15:4)*

The key to dealing with suffering is to focus on God in faith, maintaining confidence in His ultimate purposes. Indeed, faith of this nature is the key to a victorious Christian life. However, the faith must be in God and not the purpose itself. For Scripture nowhere promises to reveal God's exact purpose of suffering in a given situation. One reason God may not reveal His specific purpose is that to a person experiencing suffering, no reason would seem good enough. An honest Christian mother who had lost a child told us, "If God said to me that because of my son's death, all of Africa would come to Christ, that would not have been a good enough reason." Although God may not reveal His specific purpose in our suffering, He does give us plenty of precedents in Scripture to give us comfort and confidence that He does have an eternal purpose.

> *Oh, the depth of the riches both of the wisdom and knowledge of God! How unsearchable are His judgments and unfathomable His ways! (Romans 11:33)*

Questions for Thought

Why do you think God did not rebuke Gideon? (Judges 6:13)

Why do you think God didn't give Gideon a full explanation to his question?

What would you say, if anything, to the mother in the story above?

Suffering that God Allows for a Higher Purpose

> Drew: I once experienced a stroke followed by major surgery. I'm okay now. But lying on examination tables and awaiting the results of tests certainly brought fear. My great comfort was remembering scriptures that clearly document God's purposes for affliction. Confidence that He had a worthy purpose took away my fear.

As you review the following purposes, remember that the issue is not discovering God's specific purpose for a given situation. Rather, the clearly documented biblical causes of suffering can give us confidence that God has a worthy purpose.

1. God Allows Suffering to Put us on the Best Path

The story in Jonah 1:2-17 illustrates how God can use suffering to restore us to the correct path. God had told Jonah, "Arise, go to Nineveh the great city and cry against it, for their wickedness has come up before Me." Jonah feared that God would prove to be merciful to the people of Nineveh. Then Jonah would lose face among the people. And so Jonah ran from God. To redirect Jonah, God sent a great wind, a tremendous storm. The ship Jonah had taken nearly broke up. Every man except Jonah, who was sleeping, "cried to his god." Casting lots revealed that Jonah had brought the storm on them. Jonah confessed that he was "fleeing from the presence of the Lord." His shipmates first tried to save him. When the storm persisted, over the side into the sea Jonah went. There God sent a great fish to swallow Jonah. In the belly of that fish three days, Jonah repented of his disobedience. The fish then spit him up on dry land. From there, Jonah rejoined God's path by going to Nineveh.

Questions for Thought

Can you think of other biblical examples when God used hardship to encourage people to follow Him?

Do you know of contemporary people who turned to God in a time of trial?

How could God use suffering to turn people to Him?

2. God Allows Suffering to Build Character

And not only this, but we also exult in our tribulations, knowing that tribulation brings about perseverance; and perseverance, proven character; and proven character, hope. (Romans 5:3-4)

God could have warned Nineveh in some other manner, but He chose to use Jonah. God was committed to Jonah's character. During suffering, we may wish God wasn't quite so committed to our development. But we need to remember that His goal is to conform us to the image of His Son. God has used suffering, such as infertility, cancer, illness, depression, and sudden death of loved ones in our lives to build our character and purify our faith. Romans 8:35-39 asks the question, "Who will separate us from the love of Christ?" The verse goes on to list many types of suffering and concludes by saying that nothing "will be able to separate us from the love of God, which is in Christ Jesus our Lord." During our sufferings, we could feel God's love. And we had the joy of having Him give us an alternate purpose that reflected that love. We emerged with the heartfelt confidence that God had not and would not desert us. We learned how to persevere.

> Kit: When I could no longer make myself go on, God's love was there. When I could no longer pray, God's love interceded for me. And when I only wanted to curl up in a ball and quit, God's love allowed me to walk out of the darkness. I know that no matter what may come into my life, God's love for me will be stronger. I may

not want to go on, but His love is not dependent on how I feel. His love is stronger than the deepest pain I'll ever experience.

I have found peace in my loneliest times not only through acceptance of the situation, but through making it an offering to God who can transfigure it into something for the good of others. God does have a plan in our suffering, and it's to make us more like Him.[4] (Elisabeth Elliot)

Consider it all joy, my brethren, when you encounter various trials, knowing that the testing of your faith produces endurance. And let endurance have its perfect result, that you may be perfect and complete, lacking in nothing. (James 1:2-4)

Questions for Thought

What sort of character can suffering develop in a person?

Do you know individuals who have suffered greatly and seem to demonstrate the presence of God?

Why do you think our character is so important to God?

3. God Allows Suffering for the Good of Others

Every branch that bears fruit, He prunes it so that it may bear more fruit. (John 15:2)

Many Americans enjoy wartime movies. A frequent theme endearing to most and almost obligatory in our culture is the risk of many for the sake of an individual. For example, a WWII submarine captain might remain surfaced while being strafed and bombed as one sailor frantically paddles to safety back aboard. Miraculously the enemy misses, the sailor escapes, and everybody affirms the captain for his bravery and commitment to his men. There is no hint that the ship could have been lost with all hands and probably would have been outside the Hollywood set. Numerous "value of the individual" themes recur frequently in American literature and cinema. And somehow everything works out without the more likely consequences.

However, in real life we may be surprised to learn that God is not always like the movie captain. Scripture makes it clear that God sometimes sacrifices individuals for the good or safety of the majority. This idea is repugnant to some. It's un-American! Certainly, God cares for individuals, enough for Jesus to die for any one of us. But God will do what is best for His eternal plan.

"Son of man, behold, I am about to take from you the desire of your eyes with a blow; but you shall not mourn, and you shall not weep, and your tears shall not come. Groan silently; make no mourning for the dead. Bind on your turban and put your shoes on your

feet, and do not cover your mustache and do not eat the bread of men." So I spoke to the people in the morning, and in the evening my wife died. And in the morning, I did as I was commanded. The people said to me, "Will you not tell us what these things that you are doing mean for us?" (Ezekiel 24:16-19)

God warned Ezekiel that He would take his wife, "the desire of [Ezekiel's] eyes," to illustrate how to grieve during the Babylonian captivity. How broken Ezekiel's heart must have been. They had just one final day together, and then Ezekiel's precious wife died. Clearly, God sacrificed an individual's happiness, Ezekiel's, for the good of others. His wife lost more than happiness, her life. God used the death of Ezekiel's wife to get the people's attention. Ultimately the death of Ezekiel's wife prepared the people for the purifying ordeal by the Babylonians. That ordeal prepared God's people for His ultimate plan, the coming of the Messiah.

Joseph, Jacob's son, was indeed arrogant. But he didn't deserve to be sold into slavery by his brothers (Genesis 37). Later Joseph endured prison for maintaining moral standards. Ultimately, God used the tragedy Joseph endured to save the very brothers who had mistreated him. Joseph said, "God sent me before you to preserve for you a remnant in the earth, and to keep you alive by a great deliverance." (Genesis 45:7) God allowed Joseph to suffer for others to ultimately accomplish His plan for Israel.

Let's consider Esther, whose parents died. She was relegated into the harem of a wicked king. God caused the king to fall in love with her and make her his queen. Later Esther interceded with the king and saved her entire people. God used her tragedy for the good of others.

And we must remember Jesus, who prayed in the garden of Gethsemane, "My Father, if it is possible, let this cup pass from Me; yet not as I will, but as You will." (Matthew 26:39) If there had been a way other than the cross at that point, Jesus would have taken it. But God sacrificed even His Son for our good.

Questions for Thought

Does sacrificing for others involve suffering? Can you give examples?

Why is it hard for many to understand a God who would sacrifice Ezekiel's beloved wife?

Can you think of others in the Bible whom God sacrificed for the good of others?

4. God Allows Suffering to Teach Us

It is good for me that I was afflicted, that I may learn

Your statutes. Psalm 119:71

Scripture is clear that God will use tribulation to teach us. Affliction may sensitize someone's heart toward God in the same way that fasting can make us more receptive. We do not need to look for pain. At the same time, we don't want to waste any suffering. This sounds self-serving, perhaps. But our attitude should be that we'll try to learn the lesson God has for us the first time. Otherwise God might apply additional suffering to teach us.

> God never wastes pain. He always uses it to accomplish His purpose. And His purpose is for His glory and our good.[5] (Cynthia Heald)

Matthew 14:22-33 tells the story of Jesus walking on the water. Peter, ever bold, asked to join Jesus and had enough faith to leave the boat. Then fear of the wind and potential death stole the fisherman's faith, causing him to sink. Jesus rescued Peter and gently chided him for doubting. The experience taught Peter about faith and focus.

> *Drew:* After having endured the suffering of seven years of infertility treatments, Kit was diagnosed with breast cancer. More than five years have passed since the diagnosis and treatment. She is considered a survivor. But afterwards she surprised me by saying, "It wasn't so bad." When asked what she meant, she responded, "We had already learned how to deal with a

crisis together."

Questions for Thought

Do you think suffering can deepen our understanding of God? How?

Does suffering help us to appreciate the death of Christ on the cross?

What are some ways we can keep our suffering from going to waste?

5. God Allows Suffering to Increase our Ability to Comfort and Strengthen Others

Blessed be the God and Father of our Lord Jesus Christ, the Father of mercies and God of all comfort, who comforts us in all our affliction so that we will be able to comfort those who are in any affliction with the comfort with which we ourselves are comforted by God. (2 Corinthians 1:3-4)

Kit: One of the results of suffering in my life was the ability to comfort others. Once you suffer, you don't forget. I know how pain feels. I know what it means to have a dream go unfulfilled. And I know how to get to the other side of suffering. One temptation is to think that others can't share our pain unless they are in the same situation. Scripture says that we should be able to comfort others in ANY affliction because of God's comfort in our own life. Pain is pain and comfort is comfort. A large step in my recovery was to not give in to the idea that others can never know how much I've suffered. God has taught me that pain, to a large degree, is generic.

Simon, Simon, behold, Satan has demanded permission to sift you like wheat; but I have prayed for you, that your faith may not fail; and you, when once you have turned again, strengthen your brothers. (Luke 22:31-32)

Because Peter endured Satan's testing, he was prepared to strengthen others. Be assured that our God never wishes to waste our pain. He always desires to use it to accomplish a greater purpose if we allow Him to do so.

Questions for Thought

Have you ever been comforted by others who have gone through suffering?

Why do you suppose Peter was able to strengthen others after his own suffering?

How can God use our suffering to tenderize our own hearts?

6. God Allows Suffering to Demonstrate His Works

As He [Jesus] passed by, He saw a man blind from birth. And His disciples asked Him, "Rabbi, who sinned, this man or his parents, that he would be born blind?" Jesus answered, "It was neither that this man sinned, nor his parents; but it was so that the works of God might be displayed in him. We must work the works of Him who sent me." (John 9:1-4)

Jesus then demonstrated God's power by healing the man. Suffering of others allows us to demonstrate God's love toward those in need. We can relieve some types of suffering such as hunger with food, or illness with medical treatment. Being available to those suffering allows us to do God's works. We become God's partners in His ultimate plan. Serving others on God's behalf is a form of worship in gratitude for all that God has done for us.

Jesus tarried when he heard of Lazarus' illness. He said, "This sickness is not to end in death, but for the glory of God, so that the Son of God may be glorified by it." (John 11:4) After Lazarus had died, Jesus demonstrated God's power by raising him from the dead. The suffering of Lazarus and his sisters led to a miracle, thereby glorifying God.

> *And if children, heirs also, heirs of God and fellow heirs with Christ, if indeed we suffer with Him so that we may also be glorified with Him. (Romans 8:17)*

> *Therefore do not be ashamed of the testimony of our Lord or of me His prisoner, but join with me in suffering for the gospel according to the power of God. (2 Timothy 1:8)*

The kind of faith that overcomes the world trusts and obeys, no matter what the circumstances. The world does not want to be told, the world must be shown.[6] (Elisabeth Elliot)

Questions for Thought

What are some ways we can relieve suffering in God's name?

Why does God want us to participate in the relief of others' suffering when He could simply do it Himself?

When people are afflicted and Christians help them, what message does this give to the world?

7. God Allows Suffering as Part of His Ultimate Plan

The story of Job illustrates a part of God's "ultimate plan." Scripture records that Job was "blameless, upright, fearing God." (Job 1:1) If anyone deserved God's protection from pain, it was Job. God pointed Job out to Satan as an example of a dedicated follower. Satan replied that Job loved God because God had so richly blessed him. To prove Job's genuine love, God allowed Satan to cause Job suffering.

> *The Lord said to Satan, "Have you considered My servant Job? For there is no one like him on the earth, a blameless and upright man, fearing God and turning away from evil." Then Satan answered the Lord, "Does Job fear God for nothing? Have You not made a hedge about him and his house and all that he has, on every side? You have blessed the work of his hands, and his possessions have increased in the land. But put forth Your hand now and touch all that he has; he will surely curse You to Your face." Then the Lord said to Satan, "Behold, all that he has is in your power, only do not put forth your hand on him." (Job 1:8-12)*

Job lost his flocks, servants, and even the lives of his sons and daughters in one day. Through this suffering, Job refused to blame God. Next, Satan claimed that physical affliction would cause Job to turn away from God.

> *The Lord said to Satan, "Have you considered my servant Job? For there is no one like him on the earth, a blameless and upright man fearing God and turning*

> *away from evil. And he still holds fast his integrity, although you incited Me against him, to ruin him without cause." Satan answered the Lord and said, "Skin for skin! Yes, all that a man has he will give for his life. However, put forth Your hand now, and touch his bone and his flesh; he will curse You to Your face." So the Lord said to Satan, "Behold, he is in your power, only spare his life." Then Satan went out from the presence of the Lord and smote Job with sore boils from the sole of his foot to the crown of his head. (Job 2:3-7)*

Even in his misery, Job refused to blame God. Job's wife told him to "curse God and die." Then she left. Job's dubious friends told him to "repent" that he may be restored. Job refused to blame God or himself for the affliction. Ultimately, God chastised Job for some haughty attitudes. But Job had passed the test and proved his love. God rebuked Job's friends, revealed Himself to Job, and rewarded his faithfulness.

> *…so that you may be sons of your Father who is in heaven; for He causes His sun to rise on the evil and the good, and sends rain on the righteous and the unrighteous. (Matthew 5:45)*

God does intend to use affliction to draw men and women to Himself. In this context, He can't allow only non-Christians to suffer. Christians are going to be subject to suffering like everybody else. Matthew 5:45 shows that both troubles and blessings are distributed without merit. Otherwise, on judgment day, somebody would be able to repeat Satan's assertion by claiming, "Of course they loved You. You favored them. I would have loved You too, had you favored me." Therefore, all of us, regardless of our love and obedience for God, will share the common experience of suffering. The story of Job demonstrates how God's ultimate goodness and our genuine love for Him are being tested. This is part of His complete plan for judgment and redemption.

> It is necessary for me to be reminded that God's perspective on what is good is different from mine. His goal is my conformity to Christ, whereas often my goal is happiness and avoidance of anything that is unpleasant. To rest in God's sovereignty and His ability to cause all things that come into my life to work for good is incredibly freeing.[5] (Cynthia Heald)

Questions for Thought

Describe God's plan for you versus Satan's plan for you.

How does the example of Job fit into those plans?

Although God allows Christians to suffer, what are some advantages in this life of obeying Him?

Suffering that God Allows People to Bring on Themselves or Others

> *For it is better, if God should will it so, that you suffer for doing what is right rather than for doing what is wrong. (1 Peter 3:17)*

Any of us may bring unnecessary pain on ourselves or make suffering worse. Peter indicated that we can suffer for doing right or wrong and exhorts us to suffer for the right reasons. God created humans with a free will. Only that way could they experience the deepest voluntary relationship with Him. A free will requires the ability to make choices. Poor choices can lead to suffering. Were God to eliminate that suffering, then free will would not be all that God intends. *More than Ordinary Choices* also by Kit and Drew Coons can help reduce suffering caused by poor choices.

"Seek suffering to make you more like Jesus," some people might say by words or attitude. To illustrate their folly, we reply, "Then put a rock in your shoe." According to Colossians 2:23, deliberate self-inflicted suffering isn't effective. "These are matters which have, to be sure, the appearance of wisdom in self-made religion and self-abasement and severe treatment of the body, but are of no value against fleshly indulgence."

> *If the world hates you, you know that it has hated Me before it hated you. If you were of the world, the world would love its own; but because you are not of the world, but I chose you out of the world, because of this the world hates you. (John 15:18-19)*

The world will hate Christians for doing right. But Jesus doesn't tell us to seek the world's rejection. We have seen Christians who equate rejection by the world with devotion to Jesus. They can make themselves so obnoxious through self-righteousness and legalistic condemnation that people react negatively against them. They bring suffering on themselves. The common people of Palestine loved Jesus. The world that rejected him was the world of self-serving religious people.

Questions for Thought

Why are people not more conscience that their actions bring suffering on themselves?

Can you give examples of people seeking suffering, perhaps because it made them feel more spiritual?

Have you ever met someone who felt guilty unless they were suffering?

1. God Allows Suffering to Show the Consequences of Sin

Do not be deceived, God is not mocked; for whatever a man sows, this he will also reap. For the one who sows to his own flesh will from the flesh reap corruption. (Galatians 6:7-8)

2 Samuel 11 reveals how David failed morally as the king of Israel. He observed Uriah's wife, Bathsheba, bathing on a neighboring roof while her husband served with the army. David sent for Bathsheba and had relations with her. Later she sent a message that she had become pregnant. Since her husband was away, his un-involvement would become obvious. Implicit was a warning that David would be revealed as the one responsible. David tried to cover up by bringing Uriah home to have relations with Bathsheba. But Uriah refused to sleep with his wife in accordance to scriptural guidelines for the army. As a result, David arranged to leave Uriah exposed on the battlefield, where he was killed. David then married Bathsheba.[7] (Coons, *More Than Ordinary Challenges*)

David did not escape the consequences. The baby died. And Nathan prophesied, "I (God) will raise evil against you from your own household." (2 Samuel 12:11) David's family was subsequently divided by his rebellious sons. Don't be mistaken. Sin is serious business to God. Much of the hardship in people's lives is unnecessary. It could be avoided by following God's instructions.

Questions for Thought

Give some examples of how sin can cause suffering in a person's life.

How might God use these consequences in the person's life?

What steps can a person take to avoid unnecessary suffering?

2. God Allows Sins of Individuals to Bring Suffering to Others

Think about the previous example when David murdered Uriah. What did Uriah do to deserve death? What did Bathsheba's baby do? David's sin brought suffering to others, including the many who suffered later due to the division of his family.

> Drew: When I was ten, our family was getting ready to go bowling on a Saturday afternoon. My father was late coming home from an appointment. A police car pulled up in front of the house. My first thought was that our dog had gotten into trouble. But the policeman said to my mother, "Mr. Coons has been in an accident and he is dead." The world stopped. It seemed like everything had changed. My life would never be the same.
>
> Only years later did I think about the other side of that tragedy. A man had gotten drunk at his daughter's wedding. Driving drunk, he had killed my father and

himself. Imagine a young bride losing her father on her wedding day. Imagine every wedding anniversary remembering the sorrow of that day.

What did that young bride or my mother do to deserve that tragedy? Nothing. The drunk driver's sin affected many others.

For I, the Lord your God, am a jealous God, visiting the iniquity of the fathers on the children, on the third and the fourth generations of those who hate Me. (Exodus 20:5)

Few people want themselves or others to suffer due to someone else's transgressions. However, as part of the gift of free will, God allows people to do evil and to hurt others. Just read any newspaper to see everyday examples of people suffering because of others. Most Christians interpret Exodus 20:5 as the descendants having learned behavior from predecessors that leads to bad consequences. Although this is a difficult passage to interpret and apply, one thing is clear: God will allow individuals to suffer from the actions of others. God will hold the person causing the suffering accountable. But the suffering doesn't necessarily stop there. Repercussions may last for years, as they did in David's family.

Questions for Thought

Can you think of examples from the Bible where people suffered because of the sins of others?

What are some contemporary examples of individuals suffering because of someone else?

What are some ways that we can minimize the possibility that others will suffer from our actions?

3. God Allows Incorrect Belief to Bring Suffering

Do not be carried away by varied and strange teachings. (Hebrews 13:9)

In 1997, thirty-nine bodies were discovered. The Heaven's Gate cult, by misinterpreting biblical prophecies and mixing in New Age concepts, had convinced themselves that extraterrestrials behind the Hale-Bopp comet would take the cult members' released spirits to a higher existence. So they all committed suicide.

The Heaven's Gate example is extreme. But even Christians can bring suffering on themselves by incorrect belief. "God wants me to be happy" is an attractive belief incorrectly based on the principle of God's love. The "happy life" belief is often used in the context of decision making. Using this belief as justification, many have found themselves suffering due to inappropriate relationships, poor health choices, or financial irresponsibility. Although God offers us contentment and joy, He values our character more than our happiness.

The Bible is never wrong. But a biblical interpretation could be wrong. The Heaven's Gate cult had purchased a telescope to observe the approaching extraterrestrials. When the telescope revealed no extraterrestrials, the cult returned it as defective. They would not re-examine their belief despite evidence seen by their own eyes. By contrast, in Acts 10, early Christians believed the message of Christ to be only for the Jewish people. After seeing evidence of Gentiles receiving the Holy Spirit, they changed their minds. What we believe and use as a guide for our lives does matter. The Bible tells us in many places to seek and apply wisdom. Lack of wisdom leads to poor choices in life and likely suffering.

> *But I am afraid that, as the serpent deceived Eve by his craftiness, your minds will be led astray from the simplicity and purity of devotion to Christ. (2 Corinthians 11:3)*

Questions for Thought

Can you think of examples of incorrect belief that have caused suffering?

Have you seen Christians misuse Scripture, leading to suffering for themselves or others?

Recognizing that none of us understands everything perfectly, what are some keys to finding wisdom?

BIBLICAL RESPONSES *to Suffering*

Fortunately, God gives us straightforward ideas on how to deal appropriately with suffering. Biblical applications can minimize suffering.

> *Trust in the Lord with all your heart and do not lean on your own understanding. In all your ways acknowledge Him, And He will make your paths straight. (Proverbs 3:5-6)*

1. Give up the Right to Know Why

> *For as the heavens are higher than the earth, so are My ways higher than your ways and My thoughts than your thoughts. (Isaiah 55:9)*

Maturity is the willingness to bear uncertainty and to carry within oneself unanswered questions.[6] (Elisabeth Elliot)

When people undergo suffering, their first response is to ask why. *Why this? Why now? Why me?* As we deal with the pain, we think that if we just knew why, somehow it would all be easier to handle. But we flatter ourselves when we think, "If I just knew why this has happened to me, then it would be okay." The truth is that usually no reason would be good enough when we're in pain. And the more severe the pain, the less likely any reason would be good enough.

We can be confident that God has a purpose for suffering, and Scripture gives many of those reasons. Yet we have already pointed out that nowhere does Scripture promise that God will reveal to us how a specific purpose might apply to our situation. What reason could possibly make sense of the loss of a child, the diagnosis of a terminal disease, or financial ruin? If we were honest with ourselves, we would realize that no reason is likely good enough. To continue to demand why prevents us from healing, like a wound that is constantly reopened. Complete healing will only be ours when we put this question behind us.

> God does many things which we do not understand. Of course, He does—He is God, perfect in wisdom, love, and power. We are only children very far from perfect in anything. At times faith must rest solidly in His character and His Word, not on our particular convictions of what He ought to do.[8] (Elisabeth Elliot)

Instead of asking, "Why?" We should ask, "Who?" Who controls the entire universe? Who loves me more than anyone else ever will? Who can be trusted to give me everything I need? Those questions lead us to God, and that's exactly

34

where we need to be. We must be content to know that God, whose wisdom is perfect, has His reasons.

Questions for Thought

Why do we frequently feel like we have the right to know why?

How can an insistence on knowing why lead to frustration?

Why does giving up the right to know why lead to spiritual maturity?

2. Survival Mode

We have seen that comfort in suffering can be found through God and His servants. But healing requires more than immediate comfort. According to a report by Time Magazine[9], much of what we think about grief is misinformed. Scientific research has discredited the much-touted stages of grief and has shown that time is practically the only healer. A physical hurt to our body can be treated by a medical provider. Yet our body still takes time to heal. Like a physical injury, emotional hurt brought about by suffering or loss requires time.

We apply this insight to a concept we call "Survival Mode." There are times of suffering in our lives when all we should expect from ourselves is to survive, to go on with daily life. We must give ourselves grace and the freedom to heal on our own timetable. We need to learn how to put away our expectations of everything returning to normal and work through our pain without adding more pressure to our lives.

> Kit: Drew has often encouraged me during suffering by reminding me to just survive. If I was doing that much, he would be happy with me and God would be happy with me. This has given me the freedom I needed to put the pain behind me on my own timetable.

Questions for Thought

Have you ever had a period when just getting through the day was all you could manage?

Did you feel guilty at the time for doing so?

After a period, were you able to take a broader interest in life?

3. Be Reassured of Your Inheritance

But God demonstrates His own love toward us, in that while we were yet sinners, Christ died for us. Much more then, having now been justified by His blood, we shall be saved from the wrath of God through Him. (Romans 5:8-9)

Romans 5 tells us of the love that compelled Christ to give His life for ours. Occasionally, we learn about a person who in a crisis sacrifices his own safety to help others—a "hero." September 11th, 2001, revealed a lot of heroes. Many people are still alive because a firefighter or policeman made the ultimate sacrifice for them. Surely their life has more meaning because of the huge investment that hero made. That's exactly what God, in Christ, has done for us. Our lives have a new worth and value because of the investment Christ made on our behalf. Our lives are no longer ours alone. Our lives have a far greater purpose now.

God understands the heartbreak of suffering. God also understands the frustration and hurt we feel when others, seemingly less deserving, are blessed when we are not. "Feeling cheated" would not be too strong a phrase to describe our emotions at times. The prodigal son's older brother felt that same way after his younger brother returned home. The younger brother had left his family and wasted all of his inheritance living a selfish and extravagant lifestyle while the older brother had remained home with his father. Yet upon the prodigal's return, the father threw a party and killed the fatted calf for him, something he had never done for the older brother. Bible commentators often criticize the older brother for his attitude. The older brother was less than merciful in his reaction. However, in that parable the father reassures the faithful older brother of his inheritance. The father does not promote the younger over the older, nor redistribute the remaining inheritance.

> *And he [the father] said to him [the older brother], "Son, you have always been with me, and all that is mine is yours." (Luke 15:31)*

When dealing with suffering, some may react like the prodigal son's older brother. Maybe they've spent their entire lives trying to do the right things. Or they may have made mistakes and are trying to live for God now. In either case, it's easy for them to notice those who have no regard for God and seem to experience little suffering.

If this happens to you, remember that the father in the parable represents God. "All that I have is yours," he says. Rejoice that your inheritance with God is intact. And try to extend God's love to those who are less afflicted than yourself, even if only through prayer. If possible, try to do something nice for them. You may find that in doing so, God floods your heart with love. Your suffering is likely to feel less intense.

Questions for Thought

What are some treasures we should count on as an inheritance from God?

How can we focus on our inheritance?

Are there ways to help others who are suffering to focus on their inheritance?

4. Support One Another

Two are better than one because they have a good return for their labor. For if either of them falls, the one will lift up his companion. But woe to the one who falls when there is not another to lift him up. Furthermore, if two lie down together they keep warm, but how can one be warm alone? (Ecclesiastes 4:9-11)

If married, our spouses are particularly needed to lift us up when we have fallen. At no time does a couple need to love and support one another more than when dealing with suffering.

Life brings trouble. Being married means sharing it.[10] (Coons, *More Than Ordinary Marriage*)

Questions for Thought

Give some examples of when someone has lifted you up.

How can spouses be particularly suited to support one another?

How can church members support one another in difficult times?

5. Focus on Joy and Contentment, not Happiness

Whatever is true, whatever is honorable, whatever is right, whatever is pure, whatever is lovely, whatever is of good repute, if there is any excellence and if anything worthy of praise, dwell on these things. (Philippians 4:8-9)

In our missionary travels, we've observed that prosperity isn't necessary to experience joy. Most Africans, for example, can find joy in simple moments of life, such as singing, despite poverty. People in Jesus' time also had difficult circumstances. To them Jesus said, "For this reason I say to you, do not worry about your life, as to what you will eat; nor for your body, as to what you will put on." (Luke 12:22)

Joy can be found by heeding Jesus' words about worry. We can trust God and intentionally put away negative thoughts, especially fear. Then we are free to concentrate on the simple moments God gives. Among many things, beautiful days, warm wintertime fires, and a tasty meal are joyful moments most of us can enjoy.

Questions for Thought

Can a person really have joy in unhappy circumstances?

Give some examples you have observed or experienced.

How can the Holy Spirit give us joy in a time of suffering? (See Galatians 5:22-23)

6. Service to Others

Pure and undefiled religion in the sight of our God and Father is this: to visit orphans and widows in their distress. (James 1:27)

Drew: "If you want to feel better about yourself, do something for someone else," my grandmother would say. She could even help you to do so by assigning some chores, if needed. I always thought the good feeling that followed was relief at being finished with the work. Perhaps there was more joy at a job done for someone else than I realized. "Get your eyes off of yourself" is a well-known axiom in dealing with nearly any emotional trauma.[7] (Coons, *More Than Ordinary Challenges*)

Have you ever tried a diet plan to lose or maintain weight? Low fat, low carbohydrate, no sugar, and high protein are among many different formulas debated as to their effectiveness. Probably no one diet plan is best for every individual. But all the plans have one thing in common: "Eat less and exercise more" is the key to success. To be sure, various food combinations and other factors may be important. But ultimately all the plans involve fewer calories and more exercise. There is just no other way.

In the same manner, the way to stop thinking about our troubles is to demonstrate God's love by serving others. This is the way God made us. The most fulfilling activity is that which positively affects others, especially if it has eternal value. Like diet plans, there is just no other way.

Questions for Thought

How can serving others get our focus off ourselves?

How can having a higher purpose in life help to make our suffering seem less severe?

Have you ever experienced receiving joy by serving others when you were suffering?

7. Put Your Suffering in Perspective

Having perspective during suffering may be very difficult. However, the old adage, "I hated that I had no shoes until I met a man who had no feet," is appropriate. Regardless of how badly we feel, "suffering" is relative. It's relative to others who may suffer more severely. But it's also relative to God's eternal purpose and plan for His children. One way to gain perspective is to focus on our foundation for life.

> *And the testimony is this, that God has given us eternal life, and this life is in His Son. He who has the Son has the life; he who does not have the Son of God does not have the life. These things I have written to you who believe in the name of the Son of God, so that you may know that you have eternal life. (1 John 5:11-13)*

Drew: West Africa is known for Ebola, malaria, cholera, and unnamed fevers. While a missionary there, I contracted a strange illness. Cold crept from my hands and feet up my arms and legs. A tingling sensation followed the coldness, as though my extremities were falling asleep. At the same time, breathing became nearly impossible. Soon my whole body was paralyzed and tingling as I gasped for air. A man nearby had just died of this malady. I fearfully expected imminent death.

> In the agony of that moment, I recalled 1 John 5:13. Thoughts of eternity brought me peace. I even got excited thinking about questions to ask Jesus. But God had other plans, and I survived. Later, reviewing the unanswered questions, I felt just a little regret. Focusing on eternity has enabled me to be bold in dangerous missionary situations.

We think of God as "Our Father." And He is. However, He is a Father with an eternal perspective. God may see our tribulations in much the same manner as an earthly father sees the inoculation of a baby. A vaccination shot is painful, but insignificant, compared to a healthy life. But God is more than our earthly Father. He is also our High Commander in a struggle for the lives and souls of men. Some suffering in this world is related to the next world.

Imagine yourself meeting with Jesus while you're in a funk. "Why do I have to endure this?" you might ask. "Why don't you relieve my suffering?" Now imagine Jesus' possible response. "I died on the cross for you. Isn't that enough?" Yes! That is enough. With this perspective in mind, we can better endure the "momentary, light affliction" of this life. (2 Corinthians 4:17)

> The secret is Christ in me, not me in a different set of circumstances.[4] (Elisabeth Elliot)

Questions for Thought

Why is it so hard to put our suffering in perspective?

What are some steps to help us do so?

How can our suffering have eternal value?

8. Turn the Other Cheek

Do not resist an evil person; but whoever slaps you on your right cheek, turn the other to him also. (Matthew 5:39)

Injustice represents a particular type of suffering. Many scriptures document the importance of justice to God. Psalms 11:7 says, "He loves justice." (NIV) Because of sin, the world is full of injustice. Everyone suffers injustice at the hands of others. Injustice hurts deeply. Don't add regret to your hurt by reacting poorly.

Matthew 26:63 records that when falsely accused at trial before his crucifixion, "Jesus kept silent." Then in verse 64 after being asked directly, he simply told the truth about himself. Jesus accepted the injustice and applied his own words to "not resist an evil person." (Matthew 5:39) When personally suffering injustice, we should respond by faith like Jesus regardless of how we feel.

Questions for Thought
What are some other biblical responses to injustice?

Why is turning the other cheek so difficult?

How can following Jesus' example allow us to share "the fellowship of His sufferings" spoken of in Philippians 3:10?

9. Forgiveness

Be kind to one another, tender-hearted, forgiving each other, just as God in Christ also has forgiven you. (Ephesians 4:32)

Many verses in the Bible proclaim the importance of forgiving others. In this world, we are certain to have opportunities to forgive those who cause us suffering. Forgiveness means giving up the right to punish those who have hurt us. The surprise is that forgiveness is more for the benefit of the forgiver than the forgiven. Someone has said, "Failing to forgive is like drinking poison and hoping the other person will die." Holding onto hurt leads to anger, bitterness, and even hatred within the one who won't forgive.

Admittedly, forgiving can be difficult when we are suffering. However, the Bible is clear that we should forgive. Because we know that forgiving is God's will, we can ask God by faith to help us forgive. According to 1 John 5:14-15, God will give us the ability to forgive.

This is the confidence which we have before Him,

that, if we ask anything according to His will, He hears us. And if we know that He hears us in whatever we ask, we know that we have the requests which we have asked from Him. (1 John 5:14-15)

Questions for Thought

Do you know someone who is consumed with bitterness because they won't forgive?

Have you experienced the freedom available by forgiving others?

Is there someone who needs your forgiveness?

10. Thank God for Your Suffering

In everything give thanks; for this is God's will for you in Christ Jesus. (1 Thessalonians 5:18)

Admittedly, giving thanks for suffering does not come naturally to us. Nevertheless, giving thanks can be a tremendous demonstration of more than ordinary faith. It also reminds us that we are in God's hands and submitting to His will. Giving thanks in faith pleases God.

And without faith it is impossible to please Him, for he who comes to God must believe that He is and that He is a rewarder of those who seek Him. (Hebrews 11:6)

11. Make Wise Choices

Because suffering is a part of life, we will all face choices about the way we deal with suffering. And poor choices can bring unnecessary suffering.

> Every moment separates our lives into before and after. Some moments divide our lives into never before and always after. Many of those life-changing moments are based on the choices we make. God allows us to make choices through free will. Most awake moments include minor decisions. Some decisions are more consequential and will affect the remainder of our lives. Making good choices at those moments is for our good and ultimately reflects on God as we represent Him in this world.[13] (Coons, *More Than Ordinary Choices*)

Making good choices does not come naturally to most people. But this is a quality than can be developed.

GOD IS *good*

As we have seen, God has reasons for suffering, although He will not necessarily reveal the specific reason for our suffering. But, in our suffering, He wants to reassure us of our inheritance like the father reassured the prodigal son's older brother. Confidence of our inheritance greatly affects how we feel about ourselves. Our inheritance and our significance are like the foundation of a house, which makes the rest of the house secure. Without a foundation of faith, we have little to keep us strong in the storms of life.

We need strong medicine to diminish the effects of our suffering. We need something that is not based on our performance, cannot be taken away from us, and will not change. God's Word does just that. Psalm 139 tells us that we have value because God created us. This principle, although not new to most of us, is more important than we may realize. It sets us apart as the unique creation we are. Our value and worth are not based on what we do. Rather, our value is based on who we are and Christ's sacrifice for us.

> *For you formed my inward parts;*
> *You wove me in my mother's womb.*
> *I will give thanks to you, for I am fearfully and*
> *wonderfully made;*
> *Wonderful are Your works,*
> *And my soul knows it very well.*
> *My frame was not hidden from You,*
> *When I was made in secret,*
> *And skillfully wrought in the depths of the earth.*
> *(Psalm 139:13-15)*

Not only have we been lovingly created in God's image and freely given Christ's life for ours, but we also have a new identity. 1 John tells us that we are God's children. We have been adopted into His family and are a fellow heir with Christ. When we picture what it means to be an heir of Christ, think of an only son at the time of his father's death. Everything the father had is now the son's. Stop to imagine that! All that is God's is ours if we've made the decision to become a part of His family.

> *See how great a love the Father has bestowed on us, that we would be called children of God; and such we are. (1 John 3:1)*

Don't you wish there was a way we could be constantly reminded of these truths? Maybe a pill we could take or an operation we could undergo? Of course, there isn't one. But we can be instrumental in the lives of those suffering by reminding them of how God sees them. These truths are the solution when suffering is overwhelming us.

There is also comfort in mourning because in the midst of mourning God gives a song. His presence in our lives changes our mourning into a song, and that song is a song of comfort.[3] (Billy Graham)

In this mini-book we hoped to address the issue of doubt. What do we believe about God? Does He really care for us? Can He see our pain? CS Lewis in *The Lion, the Witch, and the Wardrobe* painted an amazing picture of God reflected in the character of Aslan.

"Is he a man?" asked Lucy.

"Aslan a man!" said Mr. Beaver sternly. "Certainly not. I tell you he is the King of the wood and the son of the great Emperor-Beyond-the-Sea. Don't you know who is the King of the Beasts? Aslan is a Lion—the Lion, the great Lion."

"Ooh!" said Susan, "I thought he was a man. Is he—quite safe? I shall feel rather nervous about meeting a lion."

"That you will, dearie, and make no mistake," said Mrs. Beaver, "if there's anyone who can appear before Aslan without their knees knocking, they're either braver than most or else just silly."

"Then he isn't safe?" said Lucy.

"Safe?" said Mr. Beaver. "Don't you hear what Mrs. Beaver tells you? Who said anything about safe? Course he isn't safe. BUT, HE'S GOOD. He's the King I tell you."[11] (CS Lewis)

God is God and He has every right to be God. He doesn't owe us a perfect life or a reason for His actions. He isn't "safe." We cannot manipulate Him, nor do we have the wisdom He has. But lest you feel completely out of control, remember that He is also GOOD.

> What comes into our minds when we think about God is the most important thing about us.[12] (A.W. Tozer)

Bibliography

1. Chambers, Oswald. *My Utmost for His Highest*. Dodd, Mead & Company, 1935.
2. Cowman, Mrs. Charles E. *Streams in the Desert*. The Oriental Missionary Society, 1933.
3. Billy Graham Daily Calendar 1999.
4. Elliot, Elisabeth. *Keep A Quiet Heart*. Wine Books, 1995.
5. Heald, Cynthia. *Becoming a Woman of Excellence*. NavPress, 1996.
6. Elliot, Elisabeth. *Passion and Purity*. Fleming H. Revell, 1984.
7. Coons, Kit and Drew. *More Than Ordinary Challenges: Dealing with the Unexpected*, 2018
8. Elliot, Elisabeth. *My Heart for God*. Gateway to Joy, 1995.
9. Time Magazine, January 24, 2011
10. Coons, Kit and Drew. *More Than Ordinary Marriage: A Higher Level*, 2018
11. Lewis, C.S. *The Lion, the Witch, and the Wardrobe*. Collier Books, 1950.
12. Tozer, A.W. *The Knowledge of The Holy*. Harper & Row, 1961.

What is a more than ordinary life?

Each person's life is unique and special. In that sense, there is no such thing as an ordinary life. However, many people yearn for lives more special: excitement, adventure, romance, purpose, character. Our site is dedicated to the premise that any life can be more than ordinary.

At **MoreThanOrdinaryLives.com** you will find:

- inspiring stories
- entertaining novels
- ideas and resources
- free downloads

https://morethanordinarylives.com/

Challenge Series
by Kit and Drew Coons

Challenge for Two
Book One

A series of difficult circumstances have forced Dave and Katie Parker into early retirement. Searching for new life and purpose, the Parkers take a wintertime job house sitting an old Victorian mansion. The picturesque river town in southeastern Minnesota is far from the climate and culture of their home near the Alabama Gulf Coast.

But dark secrets sleep in the mansion. A criminal network has ruthlessly intimidated the community since the timber baron era of the 19th century. Residents have been conditioned to look the other way.

The Parkers' questions about local history and clues they discover in the mansion bring an evil past to light and create division in the small community. While some fear the consequences of digging up the truth, others want freedom from crime and justice for victims. Faced with personal threats, the Parkers must decide how to respond for themselves and for the good of the community.

Challenge Down Under
Book Two

Dave and Katie Parker's only son, Jeremy, is getting married in Australia. In spite of initial reservations, the Parkers discover that Denyse is perfect for Jeremy and that she's the daughter they've always wanted. But she brings with her a colorful and largely dysfunctional Aussie family. Again Dave and Katie are fish out of water as they try to relate to a boisterous clan in a culture very different from their home in South Alabama.

After the wedding, Denyse feels heartbroken that her younger brother, Trevor, did not attend. Details emerge that lead Denyse to believe her brother may be in trouble. Impressed by his parents' sleuthing experience in Minnesota, Jeremy volunteers them to locate Trevor. Their search leads them on an adventure through Australia and New Zealand.

Unfortunately, others are also searching for Trevor, with far more sinister intentions. With a talent for irresponsible chicanery inherited from his family, Trevor has left a trail of trouble in his wake and has been forced into servitude. Can Dave and Katie locate him in time?

Challenge in Mobile
Book Three

Dave and Katie Parker regret that their only child Jeremy, his wife Denyse, and their infant daughter live on the opposite side of the world. Unexpectedly, Jeremy calls to ask his father's help finding an accounting job in the US. Katie urges Dave to do whatever is necessary to find a job for Jeremy near Mobile. Dave's former accounting firm has floundered since his departure. The Parkers risk their financial security by purchasing full ownership of the struggling firm to make a place for Jeremy.

Denyse finds South Alabama fascinating compared to her native Australia. She quickly resumes her passion for teaching inner-city teenagers. Invited by Katie, other colorful guests arrive from Australia and Minnesota to experience Gulf Coast culture. Aided by their guests, Dave and Katie examine their faith after Katie receives discouraging news from her doctors.

Political, financial, and racial tensions have been building in Mobile. Bewildering financial expenditures of a client create suspicions of criminal activity. Denyse hears disturbing rumors from her students. A hurricane from the Gulf of Mexico exacerbates the community's tensions. Dave and Katie are pulled into a crisis that requires them to rise to a new level of more than ordinary.

More from Kit and Drew Coons

The Ambassadors

Two genetically engineered beings unexpectedly arrive on Earth. Unlike most extraterrestrials depicted in science fiction, the pair is attractive, personable, and telegenic—the perfect talk show guests. They have come to Earth as ambassadors bringing an offer of partnership in a confederation of civilizations. Technological advances are offered as part of the partnership. But humans must learn to cooperate among themselves to join.

Molly, a young reporter, and Paul, a NASA scientist, have each suffered personal tragedy and carry emotional baggage. They are asked to tutor the ambassadors in human ways and to guide them on a worldwide goodwill tour. Molly and Paul observe as the extraterrestrials commit faux pas while experiencing human culture. They struggle trying to define a romance and partnership while dealing with burdens of the past.

However, mankind finds implementing actual change difficult. Clashing value systems and conflicts among subgroups of humanity erupt. Inevitably, rather than face difficult choices, fearmongers in the media start to blame the messengers. Then an uncontrolled biological weapon previously created by a rogue country tips the world into chaos. Molly, Paul, and the others must face complex moral decisions about what being human means and the future of mankind.

MINI SERIES

More Than Ordinary Challenges—
Dealing with the Unexpected

More Than Ordinary Marriage—
A Higher Level

More Than Ordinary Faith—
Why Does God Allow Suffering?

More Than Ordinary Wisdom—
Stories of Faith and Folly

More Than Ordinary Abundance—
From Kit's Heart

More Than Ordinary Choices—
Making Good Decisions

Visit **https://morethanordinarylives.com/**
for more information.

About the Authors

Kit and Drew Coons met while Christian missionaries in Africa in 1980. As humorous speakers specializing in strengthening relationships, they have taught in every part of the US and in thirty-nine other countries. For two years, the Coonses lived and served in New Zealand and Australia. They are keen cultural observers and incorporate their many adventures into their writing. Kit and Drew are unique in that they speak and write as a team.